THE COUP CLOCK CLICKS

ACKNOWLEDGEMENTS

It is difficult trying to remember, some thirty years after the last poem in this collection was written, all the people who provided inspiration, who encouraged and often cajoled me to write and publish them, so I ask forgiveness if anyone living or passed on is left out. Here then, not necessarily in order of their intervention, I give thanks to Kamau Brathwaite, Doris Brathwaite, Mervyn Morris, Lorna Goodison, Velma Pollard, Mikey Smith Oku Onuora, Eddy Baugh, Gordon Rohlehr, Anson Gonzales, Victor Questel, Barry Chevannes, Joe Ruglass, Tony Bogues, Rupert Lewis, Stuart Hall, Paula Burnett, Neto Meeks, Anya Lewis-Meeks, Seya Lewis-Meeks, Kwame Dawes, Colin Channer, Jeremy Poynting and Hannah Bannister. A loud and special shout-out to my late mother, Corina Meeks, for never wavering in her support. Finally, these verses would not have seen the light of day if some ten years or more ago my dear wife and partner Patsy Lewis had not excavated them from the worn and battered blue binder, typed them one by one in digital format and presented the disc to me, *fait accompli,* as a birthday gift. It took a decade, P, but here they are, at last.

BRIAN MEEKS

THE COUP CLOCK CLICKS

PEEPAL TREE

First published in Great Britain in 2018
Peepal Tree Press Ltd
17 King's Avenue
Leeds LS6 1QS
UK

ISBN 13: 978184524256

Supported using public funding by
ARTS COUNCIL
ENGLAND

CONTENTS

Part Three

Part Four

INTRODUCTION

Best known as an outstanding political scientist, Brian Meeks has been writing poems for more than four decades and is also the author of a novel published in 2003. As he says in his note on "Context", the poems in *The Coup Clock Clicks* were written between 1971 and 1988. He began undergraduate work in Trinidad four months into the 1970 State of Emergency; in Jamaica (1973-1981) he was a graduate student and later a television producer involved in "the intense process of political education, mobilization and ultimately confrontation that characterized the Manley years"; and in Grenada (1981-1983) he assisted the People's Revolutionary Government in media work and popular education programmes. He returned to Jamaica "after the collapse of an era of popular upsurge and insurrection."

Reflecting these experiences, the poems feature economic and socio-cultural division, poverty, violence, thwarted lives ("torn from / the womb /of tomorrow's / morning" (p. 32), revolutionary impulses and the countervailing activities of the CIA. The poems reprove vanity ("thinkin academically / while really peacoc / kin shirtjacs / olespice" (p. 20) and various manifestations of middle-class privilege, including conventional poetry ("plasticbushes/lookin' wild but/really very civilized" (p. 16). Tempted to write a love poem, the persona declares:

> i've always found it
> somewhat
> petty bourgeois
> to write about myself
> when so many lie out
> on the pavement

> striking for rights
> dying of hunger
> crying for someone
> to voice their plight
> and organise the fightback   (p. 61)

Meeks challenges privileged indifference. Throughout the collection, he is a resourceful poet empathizing with the poor, supporting progressive action and intimating visions of a better world. Though "mankind mows / the grassleaf / down", the poems valorize "grassroot things / the inside vibes" (p. 13). They muse on "thinkin naked", and "seein people / for themselves" (p. 19). People given at least implicit approval include Rastafarians, revolutionary leaders, and musicians.

The collection is suffused with references to music – mainly Jamaican popular music, heard everywhere: in Grenada "I-Roy, U-Roy, / Peter, Bunny, / Dennis, Gregory / even Yellowman" (p. 64). Rasta drumming is evoked "to quake a quake / inside a heart / a weakheart man / who knows not / dread" (p. 17). "The Trench Town Assault Case" recreates a heavily policed concert at the stadium, with detailed fashion notes, vivid separation of classes, and powerful assertion of Bob Marley's political importance:

> an the wings
> picked up the
> burnin an a
> lootin
> tonite
> chanted out
> the roots mans
> final blow the
> scattered bearded
> fringes skanked
> de wil' wil'
> ridim   the strange
> unnamed red glow
> could a glowed

a little briter
to 'we sick an tired
            of yu ism schism
            game'   meanwhile
down in the grander stan
de people sat an
clapped
politely.   (p. 43)

In the 1970s in Jamaica, Brian Meeks was often grouped with writer-performers such as Linton Kwesi Johnson, Mutabaruka, Jean Binta Breeze, Oku Onuora and Mikey Smith, called "dub poets" (a term resisted by some of them). They had differing creative identities, but were at one in targeting injustice and oppression at home and abroad; and they all (most often) wrote reggae-conscious free verse in Jamaican patois (Jamaican Creole) – "lang / widge is / me culcha an when / dat gaan flesh / an bone / alone leave back" (p. 29) Meeks – assured in his use of metaphor, allusion and (mainly internal) rhyme – ranges between Jamaican Standard English and a Rasta-inflected Jamaican Creole. At readings he also sometimes played the flute. The earlier poems often signal improvisation, as in jazz, breaking up words and creating extra spaces on the page. When performing in the 1970s, he would often project a sort of *dread* intentness, clarifying the rhythmic structure, speaking the poem slowly but with respect for the syntax which often rolls one short line into the next.

One of his most memorable poems, "march 9 1976", blames the United States for a lethal assault on a packed dance hall: an accountant "closes / the doors / on a stars and / stripes file." The persona's grief is nicely crafted, interweaving *"i"* sounds: "cryin i sight / brown grass / of a city / tryin to out / dry flames / with i tears"   (p. 56)

There is plenty of grief in this collection. But resilience also, and philosophical questioning:

    why do a people
        dance an
            sing

                an play ring games
                            an clap
                when the yam crop
                fails   (p. 25)

Unrealistic optimism may be critiqued by irony – "things / go better with empty redstripe / for protection / gainst irons (guns)" – but, all the same, "britelife / eyes laugh / through strong white / teeth give way / to heavy music" (p. 26). (That "heavy" suggests *wonderful, impressive* as well as *sad, weighty, burdensome*.)

   This is a collection of poems by a young political activist, mainly concerned to understand and, if possible, ameliorate the situation of others. It is also a personal memoir, shaped as autobiography. Back in Jamaica (Part 4) the persona is disappointed: people and conditions do not seem to have improved: "you get an urge to cut and run" (p. 69) but "if yu runnin from Jamaica / a hope is forever" (p. 74). A poem called "remember" is an economical roll call of fashions, places, newsworthy events, significant people, mostly leaders and musicians. The poem "sketches of spain (for Miles)" is deeply persuasive: the persona knows and loves the music. But in Part 4 the dominant mood is lamentation and elegy, most movingly in "shattered glass":

                o the three young men with hands held high
                backs against the concrete fence,
                jaws toward the sky:
                The cricket and the frog,
                the silence and the wonder
                the thunder then the silence
                and the slow motion tumble.   (p. 80)

A few of these pieces have appeared in anthologies. But here, for the first time at last, a quarter of a century after most of them were written, is a substantial collection of poems by Brian Meeks. *The Coup Clock Clicks* is an important contribution to Caribbean poetry.

– Mervyn Morris

las' rights

Gunclick/
hopefears
lovehate
the move
to make
this friday
comin' on
strong a need
to see the John
or tell the baas
jus how the cash
real low
or where the
present alms
presented every
month should go:::::
bittahsulpha
acrid lifesmell
(or how the taste of fresh white
bread upset
the bammi negrah
yam an even
though the
price is high
the saltfish
low real low)
a new
suit a tery
lene for the
weddin' next
week an Christ
masiscominthe
gooseisgettinfat
so please baas,

please put a
somethin'
in you poor
breddah hat
/Gunflash/
done

greentings

grassleaf
grounded in
mother earth
the wind blows
daily pressures
grassleaf
bends whipsnaps
down then upback
grassleaf grows
and dies
and doesnt think
but knows through
wind and rain and
other daily
grassroot things
the inside vibes
about to live:
mankind mows
the grassleaf
down

greentings two

red dust
sun baked
junk iron-bed
post out
a dust
bowl ackee
seedling declares
I life/
blue denim
striped pantslent
avoids nail
encrusted board
min' yuh bus'
down I tree
yuh know bredren
far I a watch
it grow dem las
days yah!
Joe man
membah de
coptic days
in de ol' macca
'ouse? for in
dem time
word soun
did a lick dread
seen?
youtman an
daatahs res'
away one side
IanI
eyes I-
servin'
no sight

of mud
or water
even sun
baked cracks abs
ent
widdout leaves
crabwalkin
checheh::checheh
checheh::checheh
monotonously
sunlight stirs
smoky breeze
denim eases
shifts settles
seedling grows
green leaves
sprout dust
chlorofilled,
covered broad
'ili off?' seen

dawn

i used to say
to closer
friends an
talkin' people
i write poetry
because i rhyme
down everyline
or later on
because i didn't
or made wild
wild plastic
bushes out of
letters in my mind
and had the forward
righton sense
to put them down
on paper
i used to fool
myself an friends
with plasticbushes
lookin' wild but
really very civilized:
i used to write
poetry

jus felt Count Mystic

Mankine, you know
when it hard for
words to come to
show jus how warm
a sounds can warm
inside a man a mystic
sound such as
known only before
to quake a quake
inside a heart
a weakheart man
who knows not
dread?
TUNDAHSTAAM
a boltalightnin
tree fallin
down twelve
story glass
an stressed
concrete crackin
underneath the strain
a wealth a
academic talent
runs in fear
of rusty saxes
double bass
an goatskin
drums?
or the parting
of the waves

Roas Breadfruit

(for Fanon)

jus mix ingreedy
ents one (at least)
plumpripean
freshlypicked
from off a heavy
muma (tree)
put on de heat an
pressha on a open fyah an
brimstone an don'
mek no water or
oddah coolin tings
come near de nex
fourundredyears (seen?)
tek out some (de mos' well
done) but leave de res'
an put to boil an stir de water all de time
if you tek dese out an
tek a stack yu soon will fin'
de outside black but
hook a line and dig aroun'
de inside sof' an white
an good to eat/ but
jus doan'
drop it
on de
groun
or else
it bus'
an gawn

wandalonely

was thinking
what it would
be to walk
naked
unthinkin of
how it would
be to walk naked
an seein people
for themselves
an thinkin not
of skin an
conscience
or what they
might whisper
tightly grouped
thinkin they be
together
or of people
who walk naked
thinkin naked
thoughts
was just thinkin
what it might be
to think these
thoughts without
ABC and everyone
readin it an no
one sayin i dont
understand that
shit but everyone
naked seein an
hummin mmmmmmm
cause they knew
an i knew all

these thoughts::was
jus thinkin what
it might be::::::::
no beard no pants
nohair noskin no eyes
no man peacockin
shirtjacs while
thinkin academically
while really peacoc
kin shirtjacs
olespice
whoknowswhat::::
was, you know
thinkin how it might
be to see this man
an just know he
as a man
and not dig or hate
or shout in groups
his inside peacock self
was jus tryin to see
what it might be
these wild new
ignorant thoughts
an thinkin how
it might be to
see them
as they be not
wild and ignorant
not ABC in english
language
just what they
might be
jus thinkin

monday

some
where in
a corner
of i belchin'
belly base
note plucks
dis cord
an' years
of violin
strings/other
daintycivilproper
neckhigh
suffercating
coat linings (lies)
vaseline pressd
an' neat/stif
ling even i
(not sightin'
gracetinhuts
bettycondensecups
dread wallpaper
bus up to show
what? aflowah
bloomin out
of end
less shit
a hope
(strange creacha/ting):
wind hav
ing passed
a dread
smiles
home
again

among idren
in kingstown
&other parts
of jamdown
there is much
fitin' an
division/
firstly who
naa defen'
selassie-i
a fe fall
when babylon
tumble down/
the bible also says
who eat
hog
mus
drop
so aso
seen?
firs' step
to zion
is dreadlocks
some say dread
no rasta dread
a rascal
some even a
wait for h.i.m.
to dead to
gain some satisfaction
of a kine/
correction rod
strikes down
anti-imperial

yout'
at pnp
yout'
meetn' an soul
boys reggae/penguin
blindly to a
revo. beat
(reaps more fame
than wealth)
people growin'
proteinless
no roofs or
walls/vi
lence rises/
mongst
man an man
skull&spangla
still shootin'
each other
an cleanface
redstripe/blue
bag (black)
waits his
turn to feed
again/
mongst
idren in
kingstown
jamdown
all roun
hot:
downtown
there is
strife an
argument
unity is all but absent

an yet
every
sunrise
a new day
dawnin
small black
mouths
cry out
for even u.s. people
milk gifts
an muma
looks an
hopes
no longer
to see
(in vain)
blck father/
in kingstown
jamdown
all
roun
like now

why

why do a people
          dance an
                    sing
an play ring games
                    an clap
when the yam crop
fails without
rain an the
          sunhot
dries coolside
the jangablu
stream an
          green 'guanas
dive for yel
low human piss
an black
tar bubbles shell
fumes destroyin
          twisted chicken
mesh mental
ities where skidding
crumpled safety
glass
tole us of
          doomtime
or of things
go better with empty redstripe
                    for protection
gainst irons
but more an still
          tomorrow
same again
an yet the story man
still tells

an britelife
      eyes laugh
through strong white
teeth give way
to heavy music
why

langwidge&culcha

aca
   dem
ic
name
tame
ing
hi jack
ing
daily
i spirit/
skankin
nightly
lightly
roun
neat an
cozy
argu
circle
ments of
zoo lion
steel wire
a grip
i tongue
a shape
i mout(h)
a ben'
i lip aaa
eee iii oo
…hemphazise
yu haiches yu hig
narant hidiat/
an sometime
it look as
doa you can

bus' weh
but chek again
an hope gaan
an if a had
    a wings
    a would
fly fly fly
for yu know
seh when yu
deh taak wid
dem deh
men deh
yu mus
skin yu teet
when dem kin
dem teet or
else gutta
black up slime
tomarra real
real dread
                an if it
was even original an authentic
dem tell
me
it would be easier you know
but town
dread jus a
come alf way
out de same
men mout so
dem would a
try show yu
no pas'
no fewcha
far lang
widge is

me culcha an when
dat gaan flesh
an bone
    alone leave back
an wat dreada
is when yu check
seh dis reasnin
dis said reasnin
yah
dem would a seh is
rebellious intellectual
role or sumpn so
an the screw clamps
openin slave
mouths to fuel
hunger strikes
tighten on
the bastard yout
in 72

bluwednesday

fuckery is
people in uwi
is fuckery is
people in uwi
is fuckery is
people in uwi
is fuckery
an the rage mounts
an mankine
fite to save
their balls
cos one per
cent of one
per
   cent
is much too
small
an even i
can site
that air con
dishoned grey
walls/even
bar scenes
ghetto dress/
talk/ scenes
wasnt made
for fiting
revo (soundin)
sounds cannot
willnotmusnot
stop the paper
war
   far a tru
seh some a

suffah more
dan some an
paper is a
hope
for some a
las ditch
chance
for what/
for sufferation
jus naaa stop
       so
an hidin out
in black/white tie
(shirt jac)
is jus one
bloodclaaat
          lie
so fin'
yuself
mankine cos
hidin blin'
behin yu midnite
blinders ina
'magination hide
out only killin'
you an doesnt
stop the fact
that i am dyin'
slowly
an tomorrow
too may
not be here
to cry

To a Guy I knew

but didn't meet
and for the Trinbagonians, workers and students
who feel and know what he felt
and to Carl who lies bronchial
somewhere in a living hell up Frederick street

bulleted
flesh
powdered
lifeless
stares
yout man
torn from
the womb
of tomorrow's
morning
I stand
choking
1000 crow miles
away the john
crows drool
down
the redhouse
whitehall steps
the corbeaux coolly
wait to pick
the bleached bones
of a beached
dream
long thought gone
down the storm
drain of yesterday's
volcano ::::
and the rope lengthens

the crimes/
criminals
multiply
and oilfed SMGs
belch out
black blood
and countless
unnamed who fell
before you
brother G/
sister B/
and Bogle,
Garvey,
Lumum
            ba,
Che,
Amilcar
Cabral,
will testify
for the tense
black hands
must dig
the hole
and the
hanging noose
must tighten
and the
living zombies
of this day/
nightmare
must fall-
out
in the night
light of our
tomorrow's
dawning

one love Bra Daley

how many years
of mechanics pope
menism land
hunger linstead
poco spirit
        smoking
out a ital
donkey rope
an rolled ibacco
curling roun a
ashent ashent
cosmic path
have led
to this
heights
of reasoning;
up past heavy
dubsouns
pas de science
men they try to
keep me down
inana ilaloo
a goat sure
climbin by
iserves/ an below
brita in a kina
splendid way
babylon town
dread city
under i controls
plays on
a jumpy beat/
in clouds
hidin zinc

cover faces
warm a nite
breeze/an a
kette tells
of fourteen
yout an daatahs
one more to
come nex mont
an sisD a concrete
wall long mountain
        hillside
slide down
an coffee grounded
fish an chantin
couldn wake a
sleepin spirit:
yes beardman
a long time
now been tryin
to site
de hites an
couldn fin it/
someplace up
a mountain
side a feel
a heart which
site a souns
an lik it up
real iri/
so from dis
time on a might
change a slight but
never be the same
again inside
site?
one love

Mendeville: boomtown blues and resolution

a gun court
red gash
bleeds
exhaustion
breathin
no life
breeds
mosquitos
        only
pine trees
breeze cool
music
while grassy
54° hillsides
lead down
the super
plaza hiways
into town.
johannesburg in jamaica!
sout' africa in dis yah
babylan quarta?
yes ista!
down a mendeville
when yu leave
de town pass
de col. sanders
chicken ouse
under spur
tree hill
dem ave one place
de people call wah?
johannesburg
johannesburg?
cho! yu tink seh

bevaly hills a gwaan wid anyting?
an natral de man know
who compulsory cyaah
walk pass de gate widdout
im fork an pickaxe
is true weh yu seh
iyah?
yes dread! an every
ouse res' pon

a different hill roun six
chalice load a swimmin
pool
an two soso
blackman
in de whola
place (since sixtynine
dem put dem in dem
tink it wiser
since dat time)
a bloody
alcan bauxite
gash
bleeds red mud
oozes out a
clotted future
mech
anical spades
tear down the
now vine covered
planting
ground/ roun
the corner
zinc market
lives tom
mattis

star
apple shoe
maker knitted
tams
a blood red
gash
bleeds,
breeds only
mosquitoes
mosquitoes biding
time bite thru
the lifeline
of the cholorinated
swimming pool   cool
their thirst in
the down beat
mornin
dew

The Trench Town Assault Case:
(for Bob, Peter and Bunny)

1

the gran stan wasnt really
packed to overflowin
this labour day
night.
maybe many workers
really took their
yearly rest that
day
an five dollars cya
buy saltfish now
but sure still is
a heap a
pay

2

so you know
who an who
was dere:
shirt jacs
fightin kareeba
suited double
knitted
platformed souls
battled (fiercely)
seeking seats
an eyes to
see the lates'
sunday mag
creation
strate from
out Etees
boutique

3

of course
our finest
bwoys from
duppygate
resplendent in their
labourdaybest
red stripes (well seamed)
an riotously gay
bonewhite crash
hats paraded
down the cycle
track an
battonned down
the buffer zone
of unpaid
income taxes

4

but the rebel
did come forward
a jdf us.surplus
vietnam flak jacket
aint supposed to sport
a red green an gold
seam down de side
scatterin fixed stared
mafia glasses
shadin felted
black knots
glancin down bare
out black ankles inches
from de groun
(no bells harmonize here)

5

an when the
royal party came
we didn hear
too much
confusion
out the scattered
fringes
of the cheerin
          heavin
tourism is my
bizness soulful
uptown crowd

6

the usual:
cafe au lait
white pants
white shoes
sideburns
maybe
well coiffed
afroes
image of the
new jamaica
the firs bizness
labour coa
lition in the
whole wide
world the
vip box

7

barbwire
left an rite
in de wings an
out de glare of
de gran stan
lites de
supportin cast
of not quite
thousands
for tonite
the beast has
made it very
clear
security
will be extra
tite

8

the antiparasite
wolmanized wood
bleachers appeared
quite empty
ceptin now an den
a single tell
tale fire red
glow an den again
a puff a cloud
(the lites on the hill had all gone)
out) left us to
sniff jus who
was waitin in de
blackness over
dere

an den bob came
an raped de
crowd.
no yankee inf
ested haccent
uated
guitar strum
could hide de
telegraphed ali
rite to de balls
shuffle commun
icated blow.
an the wings
picked up the
burnin an a
lootin
tonite
chanted out
the roots mans
final blow the
scattered bearded
fringes skanked
de wil' wil'
ridim   the strange
unnamed red glow
could a glowed
a little briter
to 'we sick an tired
    of yu ism schism
    game'   meanwhile
down in de grander stan
de people sat an
clapped
politely.

10

natty dread
your guitar
is a self
loadin rifle
your harmony
is a thin
black line
of resistance
natty dread
blaze out
your soun
natty dread
dont let i
down
natty dread
wail out your
soun
natty dread
dont let i
down

Cuba one

in 1962 a blue
mountain peak showed
a green horizon
to the unsuspecting eye.
standing spyglassed
staring blindly,
thought i'd see
a dull grey line
tinged with red
and barbed around/
the picture framing
captive portraits/
hiding from the sunlight/
ideologically bound.

the caribbean green
surprised my eye
and set my mind
to thinking.

did the new york
times twist the
cuban line around?
were the refugees
from trench town's
equals or refuse
from batista's hi-life
heroes of the torture
chamber, green-backed
snakes of a long-lost
hunting ground?

in 1975, marti's
children came back

into sight.
cia'ed into the present
time, lacrema milk at miles below
the current priced
brand name, meant more
than years of twisted,
tailored lies.

fidel, the workers
greet your
friendship/ those
who read between
the lines/ the unemployed
call out your name each day
on kingston's boiling side-
walks
board meetings watch
our people rise
and plan their mutual
fall in fear

in 1975
marti's children
came back into sight.
the blinds began to
blow away
for garvey's scattered
offspring waiting,
waking in the
wings.

Angola poem

Cabinda
Benguela
Lobito
Caxito
Texeira
de Sousa
Luanda

Angola
is the
baby of
new Africa.

dead heroes
Spaniard/
Indonesian,
Chilean
comrades
rise again

Angola is
the baby of new Africa.

the working
people know
no nation/
Cubans fighting
hand in hand,
Soviet workers
standing firm
mig fighters
guard the
motherland

back weh
Sout' Africa!
back weh
America!
Angola is
the baby of
new Africa.

next stop
JOHANNESBURG...

the twin barrel bucky

is a
spring
loaded
sperm
spewing
high
tension
wire
on i
titerope
of time/
watching
the gas
leak out
the lifeline
the yet
unborn
the father
figure
shines his
lovelite
out on i/
the trigger:
blu steel
heals no
wounds
    hisses
sweats out a
dialect-
ic line
     pours
down a
gunmetal
riddim

knows
no reso-
lution/
the shot:
with lead
it's said
you're as
good as
dead
with a
bucky
in you
head
if you
aint red
red red
redder dan
red
(mus dread)
the barrel:
waiting
creeping
through
the
undergrowth
of i
mind
the e-
masculated
bull
feudal-
izes
yesterday's
sunset/
the nite
knew no

end an
the people
hid in
smoky
places
daily
for
it was
tole
they say
a beast
was at
loose
an known
to be
jumpy sometimes

is culcha weapon?

can jamrock
rock out
      buckshot
shootin
jukebox souns
an beggin
for a
      ten cent
dread
for one
more stick
a ili?

will
      jamrock rock
walk naked
on Fridays
      Sundays
too   never
sleep   hunt
out the beast
haunt its thoughts
nightly
fuck his
wife on
orange st   shake
out his
lion dread
faint biznessmen
outside sheraton
fart freely?

can
     jamrock rock
crash down
a bev
     hill
          side
retainin wall
smash   plate
               glass
          torture
                    concrete
heated   headlights
crack   the   esso
sign   bend
the stoplite
signal red is
go   piss
upon the
green baize desk?

does
     jamrock   rock
know   you
               will
it shoot too
if you don't
see through
this number?

weepin an a wailin
picks you up
an spins you
roun   doesn't
want to see
you dance

jus bus
dis shot
an pick
de lock   swing de
small axe   never
sleep awhile
on sundays
while   waitin timely
once again
we smile

March 9, 1976

in a pack
dance hall
when de jump
is on
an' de muted
dub want to
eat itself
an de wood root
mix wid de
sweet scent a
ili
an de bass note
alone
stop de idrens from
flyin'
not a man tek
notice a de
yellow cortina
an de five wrench
faces inside…

circlin' 'roun'
a Burnin' Spear
number, machine gun
mentalities
centred on tripes,
everyone check
when the clappers
firs' start
dat Burnin' Spear
riddim gone
wil'…

when de fire
stop bu'n
an who nuh reach
groun' scale de
wall an de gully
outside, five
wrenches remain'
an' one lead
spattered martyr
awaitin' his medal
behin'.

down Duke st.'s
closed bound-
aries a crew cut
accountant
ticks off a
number/closes
the doors
on a stars and
stripes file.

could the golf
caddy know
who fired his life
inspired this crime
'gainst the youth
of the town?

crying i sight
brown grass
of a city
trying to out
dry flames
with i tears.

The Coup Clock Clicks

1

today
the west
burns down.
Jones town
cries out
for water.
the rat a tat
staccato/
automatic death
carves out its place
in history.
children fall
at barricades,
crumpled faces
age
before their
time.

2

roun' one
i-told-you-so's
run sour/
worker's blood
flows freely

roun' one.
confusion reigns/
reaction smiles
and files
its blade

roun' one.
the blind man
hides the facts
in Rema/
Gleaner paints
a twisted picture

roun' one.
wall street
john crows
take a closer
perch/prepare
to pick the
pieces out.

3

can ill-timed
speeches
reassuring
words
prevent the
rising beast
from
feasting?

4

in Miami
the coup-clock clicks
toward the
time...

matches lane 80: the frontline

imagine this.
a black night
no sodium light
hands on you' back
pushing you flat
the grating removed
from the drain in the
lane
no way out and no way in
terror in front
and wall to the back.
an insecure feeling leaps
into fear: sweat becomes piss:
action is etched in slow, flashing
motion: life is compressed
to a six inch ledge,
covered with shards of broken glass.
tyres screech;
guns bark;
shots whistle sweetly
like tiny mosquitos.
paint and blood;
glass and tar;
flesh and flies;
hunger and terror in
a dilated eye.
lying flat
a wall to my back
in a dark night
without sodium light

October 80 night

me an charlie an richie
an bobo an cap
tek a stack an hol' a watch
on the pitch-black roof top.
nuff shot a pop.
bobo stop watch,
me an richie get flat,
but charlie start sleep
not a peep
from him for a while.
roun' eight o clock,
pressure ease up
the radio start to crackle the news;
Kingston gone;
Clarendon gone;
Spanish Town well hot.
whol' heap a man get drop.
cap start fe bawl,
bobo him start crawl off the roof.
me an' richie still flat.
charlie? im still a sleep on im back.
hours beat, charlie stop sleep
rub im chin with expectant grin:
"who win?" im ask me an richie.
richie hol' on to im.
"we lose. dem choose de green.
is a different scene when mornin come."
charlie start weep,
I start fe cry,
no one can sleep:
bell start ring an shot still a pop.
we light a spliff an get back flat
an tek a stack, an hol' a watch
       till morning come.

personal poem no.1

Let me start these
words by saying that
i've always found it
somewhat
petty bourgeois
to write about myself
when so many lie out
on the pavement
striking for rights
dying of hunger
crying for someone
to voice their plight
and organise the fightback.
But the dialectic, not me,
decides that i write poems again
and i've tried to resist it
these last few months
and it's no use.
so, here goes.

I met you before you did me.
it was in that book,
you know,
with you defiant,
young and bold,
the image of the
baby process,
fresh flowers blooming
in a cool march morning.
even then, behind that
firm and resolute stance
i sensed, say, felt,
something soft and fragile
to be handled this side up

with care.
i'm not one to fall
for pictures
and didnt then.
It had to wait for
more than a year when
we met
in your island corner
of our common struggle,
now brashly taking
centerstage.
At first i felt as i've
told you since,
another pretty face
with nothing much behind it,
but quickly changed
my mind.
That evening on the beach
a cool breeze blowing,
your hazel eyes
confirmed my feeling
that something sweet
and something bitter
cool reserve
and sudden temper
lived together in you
in a way i felt i had to learn
and know and maybe come to
understand.
since then i've learnt,
cant say i know
what makes you what you are
to me.
i said i'd never make a woman
break down defences
carefully constructed

to weather the struggle,
built of the wrecks of
previous losses.
but here i am,
writing lines
about you.
and me.
and love.
can you imagine?

in a different stylie...

The Block-Os of St George's
play dub music
dance hall stylie:
I-Roy, U-Roy,
Peter, Bunny,
Dennis, Gregory
even Yellowman
known as 'Mr Sexy'
blaze from the boxes
of St George's on
Saturday night.
The riddim is the same
with the rub a dub
bass and the
gun shot
drum stick
bringing the guitar strum
back down to earth.
The riddim is the same
with the DJ scattin
roun' the horns
over the organ
landing flatly on the
downbeat, rising highly
once again.
The riddim is the same
but the dance is different.
In St George's hands
swing wildly,
feet skank
two-to-the-beat
two-to-the-beat,
smiles crease faces
at DJ's lewd lyrics;

no one waits for the
first shot to echo
edging in vain to the
nearest exit,
waiting tensely
for the cruel arrival
of twenty officials with automatic
fear;
feet spread widely
palms flat on zinc walls
cold metal pressed to
the base of the spine.
In St George's
they leave the Block-O's
through the entrance
walking calmly
hands swinging wildly
smiling slyly
at new conquests.
Some say its a reggae-soca fusion
or maybe just the
revolution?

october 83 dawn

the telephone tore
the wrenching silence
dried my mouth out
seared the sleep from out
my eyes.
In St George's the vulture had landed.
olive green nights and
grand anse days
the manoova and the cocoa
nutmeg and the soca
djab-djab up in Boca
Regal and Empire,
Seamoon and the akka
flashed before my mind.
what can a man do
tied to land,
rooted to his radio
watching creases creep
across his face
grey hairs sprout
as one beset with fright;
what can a man do
sweated palms,
sweated even more by the rising sun
while bombs fall
brave men fight
others die.
while long ago and
far away, o once again o once again
o once again
we cry.

Grenada

though bombs drop amnesia
and schooldays are over,
i remember.
a wood slatted bridge
and the jungle green
and the signs on every corner.
i remember
painted billboards painted stones
forward ever backward never,
a bearhug up in Butler House
a soldier serene, with his akka.
community center and wednesday's militia,
enthusiasm, full regalia,
sunday nights with Valentino, Peter Tosh
and Bunny Wailer.
a front door open through the night
running on the sand in the morning sun.
March morning on the Carenage,
glory and fever,
steel pan and soca,
Penguin, Teller and Explainer:
lambie down by Woburn,
oil dong up at Tempe,
manicou in Happy Hill,
guava, banana, tambran nectar.
pioneers playing at Heinzie school
waiting on a bus in the Market Square,
working all night and sleeping with rats
beside a printing press.
smiling hopes on every corner
too thick to harness in a
May first shower,
mother and father
son and daughter

brother and sister
come together
these i will never
forget.

returning home

what hits at first
is the hustle,
no one looks you in the eye
says hello
or smiles.
porter, pimp,
pickpocket
policeman
grimly stalk the
steaming sidewalk.
no one walks upright.
The yout you left
a year ago slowly grow
from black to grey.
hardened children
prey on windshields
wiping oily rags
for ten cent favours.
death I'd forgotten,
is no longer news.
hunger sleeps in shaded
shopfronts
nudged by passing feet,
bitten til immune
by flies
sniffed by mangy dogs
at midday
hunger lies.
returning home is bittersweet
you get an urge to cut and run.
But after night rain
morning come
pea doves fly
and air is cool

with the christmas breeze
and the blue
december sky

hustle

ten cent a race
jus
ten cent a race
Cross Roads
was his venue.
anywhere from
Carib front step
14 bus stop
underneath the clock
but preference was
for under
track price
betting shop

ten cent a race
jus
ten cent a race
guess how old.
choose any number
twenty to fifty
who can tell?
how many months
of blackened mud
and carbon
bus fumes hid the
lines
of creeping
time

ten cent a race
jus
ten cent a race
he sighed.
any horse yu wan

fe name jus tell me
who mus win
an I will chant
de bes horse race
yu eva see dis side
a town

ten cents a race
jus
ten cents a race
he cried.
some paid
some laughed
most slowed then
passed on by.
In the roar of the traffic
and the clang
of the clock
no one knew
the day he died
covered in paper
hidden from sight
by the 14 bus stop
near to track price
betting shop

remember

When I was a yout
serious soun
Desmond Dekker was aroun
Patty Pan to Lawrence Tavern
X82 to Spanish Town.
Earthman shoes an
welding glasses,
a one-foot rag out de
left back pocket,
rude was rude,
lass was lass,
gun was news an
ratchet was ratchet.

Gleaner was sixpence,
seven an' six for a pre-release;
King Tubby's, King Stereo,
Attorney Hi-Fi,
Patrick's from Papine:
the sky-juice man would chant
"yu feel de heat?"
pop a top sip a sip
was on the scene.

When I was a yout
Selassie came,
Drummond died
and Marcus came back.
Rodney grounded but couldn't stay,
right was right and
power was black.

When I was a yout
yout used to suffer

but struggled for better
(if yu runnin from Jamaica
a hope is forever)
Heptones used to fire
longshot on the wire
babylon burnin
without any water
when I was a yout
who remember?
Mr Brown an three crows in
a coffin all over town?
When I was a yout
yes iyah!
nuff yout used to
tes de fire

today

Yesterday a dreadlock died.
The flashing, prancing,
lick shot
click stop
hero sang no more.
(in the evening, no one cried.)

Today the dreadlocks chant no line.
in the heat,
hungry babies whine.
Parks and Markets
hide the slime.
gold chains tie the hearts
of men
too young to remember
Orange Lane Fire.
coke creeps up from west to east
binding wrists and blinding eyes.
miami vice asserts its
right to rule.
trash expels roots.
foreign mind meets
foreign body.
fair to white, once again
(would you believe?) is right.
In Papine, a man bares himself
to the midday crowd.
schoolers trod the dusty road
to home from school and
stone him.
Riverton smoulders in the
afternoon
Tuff Gong sleeps while Bunny
broods

Yesterday, a dreadlock died
but all that evening
no one cried

red

blood, red blood
drips
down the
door strip
settles on the sill,
slowly changing
into gel

while sprawled across the crimson floor
within
a lion mane
will flash no more.
A mystic man
lies cold
his timing all undone.

mystic man your time has gone.
A needle scratches
jaggedly, bisecting
vinyl lines
messing up my mind.

The sun is setting on
your troubled land
sleeping fitfully in
sweaty miasma
from dis three card hand.

Fear not o sleeping one
your time is done
and night is long.
But in the distance, see,
morning a come

blue black notes
still bubble on
drums still crack
an guitars strum
an weak hearts goin
scatter
when de sun hot bun.

sketches of spain
(*for Miles*)

conquistadores prance
clip, clop
across a stark Granadan landscape.
you the first from Europe
who taught us what was white
marching ragged, offstage right
into the bone-dry sunset.
Cross held in front, rampant,
setting sun, red, triumphant,
trumpeting retreat against
Napolean
Isabella and Passionara,
wringing sweat in Barcelona,
losing America,
surviving Guernica,
teaching us the word guerilla.
you the first from Europe
who taught us what was white
tilting at windmills
with martial precision:
majesty and decadence
united together,
briefly you flower, then
shatter asunder.
Listened to Miles this evening, playing your story
your mournful melody: suddenly, a shock.
In the muted horn, the walking bass, under
the snare drum's trap;
in the corner of the attic,
behind the broken clock:
The portrait of your grandfather,
beatific, smiling, baleful,
black.

shattered glass
(for Pat, Junior and Karl)

o the morning dawned calm
and the dewdrops stood
on the sidewalk grass.
the nightingales sang in Red Hills Square.
schoolchildren sat in expectation
shading in the shadow of the mountain.
mist gave way to light.

then the watchers and the waiters
the hubbub and the clatter
the engines and the horns
the fumes and newspapers:
within sight, three young men alight
hands held high
in nervous posture.

o the three young men with hands held high
backs against the concrete fence,
jaws toward the sky:
The cricket and the frog,
the silence and the wonder
the thunder then the silence
and the slow motion tumble.

o the morning dawned calm
and the dewdrops stood
on the crumpled red grass.
The sun burns hot and many more pass.
The slander and the anger
the speeches and the numbers
"accidents never reveal their path,
leaving only shattered glass".
Nobody questions

nobody asks
accidents never reveal their path
scattering only shattered glass.

Tiger

Tiger is a deejay
whose mother i knew.
like a comet, he flew
across the evening sky.
born poor in an uptown ghetto
he learnt to survive
pushing trolleys for tips
in a small supermarket,
chanting lyrics all the time.
one day Tiger made it big
and made his mother smile.
proudly she would say:
"is my boy tiger dat, the bes'
deejay in the whola J-A".
he toured America,
jazzed flashy pendants
and painted his name on his
shiny Toyota.
i met him once in front the stage;
people loved him, tore his clothes:
girls went crazy over tiger.
in the press all i remember,
a golden grin and shining eyes.
i went away and on return, once again
i saw his ma. This time, she cried.
Tiger she felt had picked up a habit
which, she feared, could make him die.
in the months to come, Tiger's star
declined. His name no longer on the charts,
he didn't make the headlines.
but those who cared could glimpse his car,
rusting round the rims,
weaving its way through the uptown snarl,
never in the line.

old deejays never die they say,
they simply settle, then
fade away.

Reading at Second Hermitage Cultural Days, July 1975

CONTEXT

These poems were all written between 1971 and 1988 and fall into four distinct phases of what, only fully grasped in retrospect, was my youth. In 1970 I went to Trinidad to attend the University of the West Indies, (UWI) St Augustine campus. I arrived there in September, some four months into the State of Emergency that was declared to quell an intense period of popular black power demonstrations from February through April of that year. On the declaration of the State of Emergency on April 22, young officers in the Trinidad and Tobago regiment led a mutiny in solidarity with the black power movement, but then surrendered to loyalist soldiers before it had really gained momentum. My undergraduate years from 1970-1973 were filled with echoes of these events and what came to be known as the 'February Revolution' which was further reinforced when many of the detainees were released from prison, and by the existence of a small but persistent guerrilla insurgency that developed among radicalized black power supporters – the National United Freedom Fighters (NUFF).

I left Trinidad and returned home to Jamaica in 1973, where Michael Manley's People's National Party (PNP) government had come to power a year earlier and where, over the next eight years, the PNP would move inexorably to the left of its mildly Fabian socialist positions to adopt increasingly radical anti-imperialist agendas. I was a graduate student at the UWI Mona and later a television producer at the government-owned Jamaica Broadcasting Corporation (JBC) and very much involved as both participant and observer in the intense process of political education, mobilization and ultimately confrontation that characterized the Manley years. Indeed, in 1980, shortly after achieving victory in the bloody 1980 general elections, the conservative Jamaica Labour Party (JLP) leader and Prime Minister elect Edward Seaga declared that one of his major objectives was to clean out the JBC of pro-Manley elements and he was true to his word, declaring the entire News and Current Affairs department and myself among them, redundant early in 1981.

Later that year, I left for Grenada, where I had been asked to play a role in building the media from the leadership of the People's Revolutionary Government (PRG) which had toppled the Eric Gairy regime in that country only two years before. I worked in Grenada in the radio station and the Free West Indian newspaper as well as on popular education programs until September 1983, when I returned to Jamaica to start work on my doctoral dissertation, which I thought would be on the political economy of the still thriving Grenadian Revolution. However, two weeks after leaving, the People's Revolutionary Government collapsed with the tragic killing of Prime Minister Maurice Bishop and a number of his closest associates, immediately followed by the US-led invasion.

The poems then, roughly follow this turbulent yet extraordinarily rich period of Caribbean history in which I was privileged to come of age. The first group, from "Las rights" through to "To a guy I knew", were written during my Trinidad sojourn; "one love bra Daley" to "October 80 night" were written during or about the Seventies in Jamaica; "personal poem no1" to "Grenada" reflect on my two years in the People's Revolution and the last group, from "returning home" to "Tiger" concern themselves with the new, strange, yet also oddly familiar world of Jamaica following the collapse of an era of popular upsurge and insurrection.

GLOSSARY

Akka: Grenadian for Soviet AK47 assault rifle

Bammi: Jamaican cassava bread

Betty condense cups: Using tins of a popular brand of condensed milk as a cup, a sign of poverty

Bevaly Hills: Wealthy community on hill overlooking Kingston

Block-Os: Eastern Caribbean term for block parties

Blue Bag: Island Special Constabulary Force (lower ranked police with blue seamed trousers)

Bra Daley: Late Leonard Daley, considered one of Jamaica's leading "Intuitive" (untrained) artists

Cabinda, Benguela etc: Angolan towns made popular as reported in the Angolan Civil War

Chalice: Rastafari term for water-cooled marijuana/ganga pipe

Cho: Jamaican exclamation of surprise/disdain.

Clappers: Fireworks, gunshots

Corbeaux: Vultures (Trinidad)

Count Mystic: Compression of Count Ossie and the Mystic Revelation of Rastafari

Crabwalkin: Early Seventies reggae dance style.

Djab Djab: Devil masquerade in Eastern Caribbean carnival

Drummond: Late Jamaican trombonist, Don Drummond

Gleaner: Oldest Jamaican daily. Conservative and hostile to Manley's PNP in the Seventies

Gracetinhuts: Popular tinned products flattened and utilised for roofing material in slum communities – Grace Kennedy is one of the longest established Jamaican food-processing companies.

Grand Anse: Popular Grenadian beach

Guy: As in "To a Guy I knew…" Guy Harewood, leader of the National United Freedom Fighters (NUFF) and killed in a shootout with the Trinidad police in October, 1973

Idren(s):   Rastafari for brethren, close friend

Ili:	marijuana, ganja, herbs
I-Roy, U-Roy:	Jamaican deejays and singers popular in the 1970s
Jamrock:	Used variously for Jamaica or Jamaican music
JDF:	Jamaica Defence Force
John Crow:	Turkey vulture (Jamaica)
Kareeba:	Formal dress. A Seventies Jamaican alternative to the western suit.
Lacrema:	Cuban brand of condensed milk, donated to Jamaica for hurricane relief in the seventies
Lambie:	Conch (Grenada)
Lass:	Cutlass
Manicou:	Small marsupial, eaten and considered 'wild meat' in Eastern Caribbean
Manoova:	Military maneuvers practiced by the people's revolutionary Army and people's militia in anticipation of possible invasion attempts during the Grenadian Revolution
Matches Lane:	PNP supportive enclave next to the large JLP stronghold of Tivoli Gardens in Western Kingston. Thus on the frontline of the internecine battles of the Seventies
Mendeville:	Rastafari derogatory distortion of Mandeville, a Jamaican hill town, made prosperous (for some) by the bauxite and alumina industry
Mr Brown:	Myth that circulated in Kingston in the early Seventies that there was a coffin that was moving around the city with three crows on top who were asking for a Mr Brown
Negrah Yam:	Negro Yam, variety of Jamaican yam
Oil dong (down):	Dish made of salt meat, breadfruit, coconut milk and bananas (Grenadian)
Orange Lane Fire:	Horrific Fire leading to deaths of many during the wars of the Seventies
Passionara:	La Passionara, communist heroine of the Spanish civil war
Patty pan:	Small bus used to ply hilly routes

Penguin: Popular funk-related dance of the seventies

Penguin, Teller and Explainer: Trinidadian and Grenadian calypsonians

Poco: Pocomania (pukumina). African Jamaican religion.

Popemenism: Derogotary Rastafari reference to Roman Catholicism.

Ratchet: Ratcheted knife, similar to a switch blade and popular among "rude bways" in Jamaica in the Sixties

Red Stripe: Jamaica Constabulary police force (regular police with a red stripe on their trousers)

Red: High following the smoking of ganja

Red House: Home of Parliament of Trinidad and Tobago

Rema: Inner-city community in South St Andrew, supportive of the JLP in the Seventies

Riverton: Largest dump in Kingston and notorious for blazing out of control

Rodney: Walter Rodney, Guyanese-born historian whose exclusion from returning to work in Jamaica in 1968 led to famous demonstrations and rioting

Shirtjac: Formal shirt. An alternative to the jacket and tie

Skank: Sixties and Seventies Jamaican for stealing. Also a dance style

Skull&Spangla: Sixties Jamaican urban street gangs

Sky Juice: Shaved ice and syrup, served in a paper cone

SMG: Sub Machine Gun

Trash: Eighties Jamaican for nattily dressed

Trinbagonians: Synthetic name for citizens of Trinidad and Tobago. Emerged in the black power period

Tuff Gong: Bob Marley's nick name

Whitehall: Office of the Prime Minister in Trinidad

Woburn, Tempe, Happy Hill: Grenadian townships

ABOUT THE AUTHOR

Brian Meeks is Professor of Africana Studies and Chair of the Africana Studies/Rites and Reason Theatre Department at Brown University. He has authored or edited twelve books on Caribbean politics, political culture and thought, including *Caribbean Revolutions and Revolutionary Theory* (1993 and 2000), *Culture, Politics, Race and Diaspora: the Thought of Stuart Hall* (2007), and *Critical Interventions in Caribbean Politics and Theory* (2014). His novel *Paint the Town Red* was published by Peepal Tree in 2003. Before coming to Brown in 2015, he served for many years at the University of the West Indies in the Department of Government and as Director of the Sir Arthur Lewis Institute of Social and Economic Studies and Director of the Centre for Caribbean Thought at the University of the West Indies, Mona, Jamaica.

Mervyn Morris is a poet and professor emeritus at the University of the West Indies, Mona, Jamaica. In 2014, he became Jamaica's first poet laureate since Independence.

ALSO BY BRIAN MEEKS

Paint the Town Red
ISBN: 9781900715744; pp. 120; pub. 2003; £7.99

Brian Meeks' novel is a moving requiem for the years of an extraordinary ferment in Jamaican society, when reggae and Rastafarian dreams reached from the ghettoes to the University campus, and idealistic young men and women threw themselves into the struggle to free independent Jamaica from its colonial past. In portraying the the temptations towards tribal revenge that corrupted the vision of change, Meeks' sensitive and insightful novel speaks powerfully to the present, when even in the recent past, Jamaica's political divisions have erupted into killings on the streets.

As Mikey Johnson takes a minibus through Kingston on his release from eleven years in jail, what he sees and the persons he meets provoke memories of the years when those who sought to destabilize Jamaican society, fearful of the radical socialist direction it was taking, unleashed a virtual civil war. His encounters reveal that few escaped unscathed from those years: there are the dead (in body and in spirit), the wounded, the turncoats, and those like himself who are condemned to carry the burden of those times.

Mikey's quest to discover why he survived when his friend Carl and lover, Rosie, were killed in a shootout with the police draws him to look for Caroline, the other woman he was involved with before his imprisonment. From her he discovers a bitter truth about Jamaica's unwritten code of class and its role in his survival.

One of Mikey's encounters is, we learn in a postscript to the novel, with Rohan, Rosie's brother. Rohan has suffered this loss deeply, but has survived to move forward, while Mikey, with the stigma of his imprisonment, is trapped in the past. It is Rohan who tells Mikey's story, a revelation that casts a reflexive light on the relationship between the writer and his subject.